LIGHT AND SHADOWS
Selected Poems and Prose

Juan Ramon Jimenez

Translated by
Robert Bly, Dennis Maloney,
Antonio T. de Nicolas, James Wright, and Clark Zlotchew

Edited by Dennis Maloney

WHITE PINE PRESS

ISBN 0-934834-72-5

Acknowledgements
Translations by Robert Bly reprinted from *Selected Poems of Jimenez and Lorca*, a Beacon/Sixties Press Book, with permission of Robert Bly
Translations by Dennis Maloney reprinted from *Naked Music: Poems of Juan Ramon Jimenez*, White Pine Press
Translations by James Wright reprinted from *Collected Poems - James Wright*, Wesleyan University Press, with permission of Wesleyan University Press
Translations by Antonio T. de Nicolas reprinted from *Platero and I*, Paragon House Publishers, with permission of Paragon House Publishers

This publication was made possible, in part, by a grant from the New York State Council on the Arts.

Cover by Elaine LaMattina

Designed by Watershed Design

Published by White Pine Press
        76 Center Street
        Fredonia, New York 14063

CONTENTS

POEMS

The Lumber Wagons...................................9
Winter Scene (Snow)................................10
Green...11
As In the Motionless River........................12
New Leaves..13
Yellow Spring.....................................14
The Wrong Time....................................15
Nothing More?.....................................16
Nocturne..17
Dreaming..18
How Close to Becoming Spirit Something Is.........18
Moguer..19
On the City Ramparts of Cadiz.....................19
Stormclouds.......................................20
Sky...20
Rose of the Sea...................................21
I Took Off Petal After Petal, As if You Were a Rose...21
Rosebushes..22
Cemetery..22
Deep Night..23
An Imitator of Billy Sunday.......................24
Author's Club.....................................25
Walt Whitman......................................26
Lavender Windowpanes and White Curtains...........27
Nocturne..28
Remorse...29
Convexities.......................................29
Smoke and Gold....................................30
Nocturne..31
Intelligence, Give Me.............................31
Sleep is Like a Bridge............................32
Oceans..32
I Am Like a Distracted Child......................32
To the Bridge of Love.............................33
Road..33
I Pulled on the Reins.............................33
At First She Came to Me Pure......................34
I am Not I..34
Life..35
The Poem..35
New Cold..35
Dawn..36
To Dante..36

Ideal Epitaph for a Sailor........................37
The Ship, Solid and Black........................37
What an Immense Rip..............................38
Facing the Virgin Shadow.........................38
Figurations......................................39
Memory-4...39
Memory-5...40
To Beloved Old Age...............................40
Uphill...41
Light and Water..................................41
Song...42
Even Though My Soul Fits So Wonderfully..........42
Butterfly of Light...............................42
Full Moon..43
Dusk...43
Dawn Outside the City Walls......................44
Peace..45
With the Roses...................................46
Full Consciousness...............................46
I Wish That All My Poems.........................47

From *Platero and I*

Prologue...51
Platero..52
Games at Dusk....................................53
The Eclipse......................................54
Kindergarten.....................................55
Figs...56
The Gelding......................................57
The Terrace......................................58
Return...59
Don Jose, the Priest.............................60
The Cistern......................................61
The Little Cart..................................62
Bread..63
Darbon...64
Friendship.......................................65
The Tree in the Corral...........................66
The River..67
The Old Fountain.................................68
Pine Nuts..69
The Fable..70

INTRODUCTION

Juan Ramon Jimenez is a poet of solitude and lightness. His poems are ecstatic moments of life which rise up like sparks from a campfire. Rather than relying on rhythm and technique, he emphasised how a poet should live, realizing that only in solitude do man's emotions finally become clear to him.

Born in Andalucia, Spain in 1881, he moved to Madrid after his youth and was one of the early inhabitants of the Residencia de Estudiantes, the home of many of Spain's great poets early in the century. In 1900, at the age of 18 he began participating actively in Spanish literary life. Jimenez's health was always frail and from the age of twenty he spent the next several years in and out of sanitoriums. He continued to write and in 1907 moved back to the country and wrote several books of poems and his well-known prose work, *Platero and I*. In 1913 he returned to the capital and met Zenobia Camprubi, his future wife. His journey from Spain to America to marry her in 1916 is recorded in his book *Diary of a Poet Recently Married*.

Juan Ramon Jimenez, along with Antonio Machado and Unamuno formed the generation of '98 which ushered in a renaissance in Spanish poetry at the turn of the century. The work of Jimenez and Machado in particular inspired the next generation of Spanish poets including Lorca, Aleixandre, Alberti, and Guillen. Juan Ramon, as he was fondly known, was very supportive of younger writers, commenting on their work and publishing it in magazines he edited.

With Lorca, Hernandez and Machado dead in the wake of the Spanish Civil War, Jimenez, like many other poets, musicians, and painters left Spain, living first in America for several months, before settling in Puerto Rico, where he lived until his death in 1958.

In 1956 Jimenez received the Nobel Prize for Literature. In awarding the prize the Nobel Committee honored Jimenez "for your lyric poetry, which in the Spanish language, constitues an exemplar of high spirituality and artistic purity" and said, "By being an idealist dreamer, Jimenez represents... the highest Spanish tradition, and honoring him is also honoring Machado and Garcia Lorca..." The joy of receiving the Nobel was diminished by his intense sadness and grief over his wife, who was on her deathbed when he received news of the prize. She died shortly after, and Jimenez stopped writing, living himself only until 1958.

Juan Ramon Jimenez began his artistic life as an impressionistic style painter but this soon gave way to writing. His poetry retained this impressionistic quality, however, in its reliance on sensations of the eye, ear, touch, movement, smell, and in the use of color. He constantly attempted to articulate his vision using words as if they were paint, utilizing an economy of language to produce an impressionistic effect.

Jimenez dedicated over 50 years of his life to poetry. To Juan Ramon each poem had a life of its own, a bit of the Tao running through it. He seems to have gradually become aware of the natural force residing in all things, a tree, a woman, a moonlit mountain...

Juan Ramon strove for what he called naked poetry, a poetry near emotion:

> Music,
> a naked woman
> running mad through the pure night

(translated by Robert Bly).

In another poem Jimenez uses the metaphor of a girl. The girl first comes to him clothed in the innocence of a child, but soon begins to dress in the clothes of a queen and he grows to hate her, not knowing why. Only when she begins to undress could he smile on her again; at last she appears naked, "poetry, naked and mine forever."

The idea for this collection developed two years ago from the realization that the work of Juan Ramon Jimenez was virtually out of print and unavailable in English translation. The only poetry in print was a small pamphlet of fourteen poems I translated some years ago.

This collection brings together those poems along with translations by poets Robert Bly and James Wright and a group of new translations done for this volume by my friend and colleague Clark Zlotchew and myself. To the poems we have added a generous selection from Juan Ramon's widely admired prose work *Platero and I*, translated by Antonio de Nicolas, to provide a rounded introduction to the work of Jimenez. I would like to thank the poets, translators, and original publishers for permission to reprint their work.

Happily, the availability of Juan Ramon's work in English has improved substantially. Paragon House Publishers (2 Hammarskjold Plaza, New York, N.Y. 10017) has committed itself to publishing several volumes of poetry and prose by Jimenez over the next several years, all translated by Antonio de Nicolas. They have already published two books of prose, *Platero and I and Stories of Life and Death*, and recently issued the first of their bilingual poetry collections, *God Desired and Desiring*. Later in 1987 they will issue two additional collections of poetry, *Invisible Reality* and *Space/Time*.

POEMS

Translated by
Robert Bly, Dennis Maloney,
James Wright, and Clark Zlotchew

THE LUMBER WAGONS

The lumber wagons are already there.
—The pines and the wind have told us,
the golden moon has told us,
the smoke and the echo have told us . . .
They are the carts that go by
in these afternoons at dusk,
the lumber wagons carrying
the dead trees down from the mountain.
What a sound of crying from these carts
on the road to Pueblo Nuevo!
The oxen came along
in the starlight, daydreaming
about their warm stalls in the barn
smelling of motherhood and hay.
And behind the lumber wagons
the ox-drivers walking,
the ox-prod on their shoulders,
and eyes watching the sky.
What a sound of crying from these carts
on the road to Pueblo Nuevo!
The dead trees as they move
through the calm of the fields
leave behind a fresh honest smell
like a heart thrown open.
The Angelus falls
from the steeple of the ancient town
over the stripped fields
which smell like a cemetery.
What a sound of crying from these carts
on the road to Pueblo Nuevo!

R. B.

WINTER SCENE (SNOW)

Where have all the colors hidden themselves
on this black and white day?
The leaf black, the water grey, the sky
and earth, a pale white and black,
and the melancholy city
of a romantic's old etching.

The man walking is black;
the startled bird is black
darting through the garden like an arrow . . .
Even the silence is hard and faded.

Evening approaches. The sky
is not gentle. In the sunset,
a vague yellow, almost glowing,
almost not. In the distance, fields
the color of dry iron.

                And night descends like
a burial; wrapped in black
and cold, starless, all white
and black, like the black and white day.

                                        D.M. & C.Z.

GREEN

Green was the girl.
Green eyes. Green hair.

Her wild rose
was neither red nor white, but green.

Through the green air she came!
(The whole earth turned green.)

Her shining foam
was neither blue nor white, but green.

Over the green sea she came!
(Even the sky turned green.)

My life will always leave
a small green gate open for her.

D. M.

AS IN MOTIONLESS RIVER

As in motionless river, on the paper, my forehead,
motionless, reflects the words
that vibrate in its sky, like the notes of stars
lost in a labyrinth of bells.

Notes that gradually form, light by light, sound by
sound, rose by rose, tear by tear,
a new architecture bright and singing,
softened by the moonlight of my soul.

Endless end of a broken and nameless harmony,
never extinguished in thought;
dry leaves, colored glass, unique flowers,
which intertwine in the shadows.

Something unknown, from beyond, that comes into our
lives along transformed paths,
like a wandering dawn, which in skies of dream
scatters behind silver pollen.

D.M. & C.Z.

NEW LEAVES

to Isoldita Espla

Look, by the silver poplars,
how the golden children climb to the sky!

And they go looking at the sky,
raising their eyes into the blue,
    like pure dreams.

Look, by the silver poplars,
how the golden children climb to the sky!

And the blue of their beautiful eyes
and the sky are touching . . .
    eyes and sky are one!

Look by the silver poplars,
how the golden children climb to the sky!

Don't run, go slow
it is only into yourself
        that you must go!

Go slow, don't run
for the child of yourself, just born
eternal
cannot follow!

D. M.

YELLOW SPRING

April came, all
full of yellow flowers.
The yellow stream,
the yellow fence, overflowing,
the children's cemetery,
the garden where love was living.

The sun anointed the world with yellow,
with falling light.
Ah, through the golden lilies,
the warm golden water;
the yellow butterflies
above yellow roses!

Yellow garlands were climbing
the trees, the day
was a grace perfumed with gold
in a golden awakening of life.
Among the bones of the dead,
God opens his yellow hands.

D. M.

THE WRONG TIME

I set my heart ahead,
as if it were a clock,
towards a tranquil moment.

But happiness did not ring out
(happiness was in its place
and that ruse was foolish),
and it never was the exact time!

(Reality, confused, was
already living in the previous hour
of that hopelessness.)

With what sorrow I set back
your time, restless heart!

D.M. & C.Z.

NOTHING MORE?

Only my face and the sky.
The only universe.
My face, alone, and the sky.

(Between them, the pure breeze,
a fond caress, the only hand
that brings so much plentifulness;
the breeze, always rising and falling.)

Above me, all that is life,
the entire dream within me,
brushing against my senses with its wings,
that he has brought into harmony.

Nothing more.
                    Are you perhaps
the breeze that comes and goes
from the sky, love, to my face?

D.M. & C.Z.

NOCTURNE

O, sea of unknown waves
without stations or stops,
water and moon, no more, night after night!

I remember my land,
which belonged to others but also to me,
when I passed through on the night train,
through the places themselves, at odd hours
of previous years . . .

     —Distant mother,
Sleeping land,
with firm and constant arms,
with a peaceful lap
—tomb of eternal life
with the same adornments restored—
mother earth, who always
waits in your only
truth for the sad glances
of the wandering eyes!—

. . . I remember my land:
the olive groves at dawn,
standing firm before the white,
rose, or yellow moon,
awaiting the return
of those who, without belonging to you or owning you,
loved you and loved you . . .

D.M. & C.Z.

DREAMING

—No, no!
and the dirtyneck boy starts crying and running
without getting away, in a moment, on the streets.
His hands,
he's got something in his hands!
He doesn't know what it is, but he runs to the dawn
with his hidden prize.
Endlessly beforehand, we know what his trophy is:
something ignored, that the soul keeps awake in us.
We almost start to glitter inside his gold
with extravagant nakedness . . .
—No, no!
and the dirtyneck boy starts crying and running
without getting away, in a moment, on the street.
The arm is strong, it could easily grab him . . .
The heart, also a beggar, lets him go.

J. W.

How close to becoming spirit something is,
when it is still so immensely far away
from hands!
like starlight,
like a nameless voice
in a dream, like faraway horses,
that we hear, as we breathe heavily,
one ear placed to the ground;
like the sea on the telephone . . .
And life begins to grow
within us, the delightful daylight
that cannot be switched off,
that is thinning, now, somewhere else.
Ah, how lovely, how lovely,
truth, even it is not real, how lovely!

J. W.

18

MOGUER

Moguer.   Mother and brothers.
The house, clean and warm.
What sunlight there is, what rest
in the whitening cemetery!
In a moment, love grows remote.

The sea does not exist; the field
of vineyards, reddish and level,
is the world, like a bright light shining on nothing.
and flimsy, like a bright light shining on nothing.

    Here I have been cheated enough!
Here, the only healthy thing is to die.
This is the way out, that I wanted so badly,
that escapes into the sunset.

Moguer.   If only I could rise up, sanctified!
Moguer.   Brothers.and sisters.

                                        J. W.

ON THE CITY RAMPARTS OF CADIZ

The sea is enormous,
just as everything is,
yet is seems to me I am still with you . . .
Soon only water will separate us,
water, restlessly shifting,
water, only water!

                                        J. W.

Stormclouds
give their morose faces to the sea.

The water, worked up out of iron,
is a hard, flat landscape,
of exhausted mines,
in a state of collapse,
ruins.

Nothingness! That word, for me,
here, today, comes home,
the cadaver of a word,
laid out, naturally,
in its own grave.
                    Nothingness!

                                        J. W.

SKY

I had forgotten you,
sky, and you were nothing
more than a vague existence of light,
seen without name,
by my weary, lazy eyes.
And you would appear, among the idle
discouraged words of the traveler,
like a series of tiny lagoons
seen in a watery landscape of dreams . . .

Today I gazed at you slowly,
and you are rising as high as your name.

                                        D.M. & C.Z.

20

ROSE OF THE SEA

The white moon takes the sea away from the sea
and gives it back to the sea. Beautiful,
conquering by means of the pure and tranquil,
the moon compels the truth to delude itself
that it is truth become whole, eternal, solitary,
though it is not so.
                        Yes.
                              Divine plainness,
you pierce the familiar certainty, you place
a new soul into whatever is real.
Unpredictable rose! you took the rose away
from the rose, and you could give back
the rose to the rose.

                                                        J. W.

I took off petal after petal, as if you were a rose,
in order to see your soul,
and I didn't see it.

However, everything around—
horizons of fields and oceans—
everything, even what was infinite,
was filled with a perfume,
immense and living.

                                                        R. B.

21

ROSEBUSHES

It is the sea, in the earth.
Colors of the south, in the winter sun,
contain the noisy shiftings
of the sea and the coasts . . .
Tomorrow in the sea!—I say, rather, in the earth
that moves, now, into the sea!

J. W.

CEMETERY

This tiny village of dead people has stayed on, forgetfulness which is remembered, in the care of some trees that in their rural childhood were large, and now that they are old, are small, among the frightening skyscrapers. Now the night makes the living who are asleep a little higher up, parallel with the dead who are asleep a little lower down, a little time that is past and a little time to come. Parallel rows toward a neighborly infinity, though in it they will never meet!

The wind removes and puts back the snow from the gravestones, blinding me with its sharp whiteness, changing colors in its high whirling columns in the light of the white streetlamps. The hours make the darkness more apparent, and whatever was resting in the daylight is awake now, and looks, listens, and sees. In this way the dreams of these dead people are heard, as if they were dreaming out loud, and their dreaming over so many years, more alive than the dreaming of those dead for one night, is the life that is highest and deepest in the abandoned city.

R. B.

DEEP NIGHT

New York deserted—without a person! I walk down Fifth Avenue, with lots of time, singing aloud. From time to time, I stop to look at the gigantic and complicated locks in the bank, the department store windows being changed, the flags flapping in the night . . . And this sound which my ears, as if inside some enormous cistern, have taken in unconsciously, coming from I don't know which street, gets nearer, harder, louder. The sounds are footsteps, shuffling and limping, they seem to be coming from above, they constantly approach and never manage to get here. I stop again and look up the avenue and down. Nothing. The moist spring moon, with circles under its eyes, the sounds, and I.

Suddenly, I can't tell if far off or near, like the solitary soldier I saw on the sands of Castille, that evening when the sea wind was strong, a point or a child, or an animal, or a dwarf—What? And slowly it comes closer. Closer. About to pass. I turn my face and meet his gaze, the eyes bright, black, red and yellow, larger than his face, all he is is his gaze. An old Negro, crippled, with a shrunken overcoat and a hat with a faded top, greets me ceremoniously, and then, smiling, goes on up Fifth Avenue . . . A brief shudder goes through me, and with my hands in my pockets I go on, the yellow moon in my face, half singing to myself.

The echo of the crippled Negro, king of the city, makes a turn around the night in the sky, now toward the west.

R. B.

AN IMITATOR OF BILLY SUNDAY

Billy Sunday, the fear-inspiring preacher, does not dare to come to this "city of heathens." However, he has disciples with a certain relative "power." One of these is Pastor A. Ray Petty, of the Anabaptist Church in Washington Square. Here are two of his public announcements:

Notice in "C"

THE CRISES OF CHRIST

Organ Recital 7:45 P.M.

Preaching 8 P.M.

SPECIAL SUNDAY EVENING SERVICES

A. RAY PETTY

Topics:

April	2.	Christ and the crowd
April	9.	Christ and the coward
April	16.	Christ and the cross
April	23.	Christ and the conquest
April	30.	Christ and the crown

SPECIAL MUSIC   GOOD SINGING

YOU ARE WELCOME

Notice in "Sportsman":

BASEBALL SERMONS

Sunday evening at 8 P.M.

A. Ray Petty, Pastor

Topics:

May 14.	The pinch hitter
May 21.	The sacrifice hit
May 28	Game called on account of darkness

LIVE MESSAGES   HOT OFF THE BAT

A spring night. Washington Square green, the sky still faintly gold from the day which was hot and dusty; the moon moves like a bird made of the light from tree to tree; the air is moist from jets of water whose tips are sheared off by the gusty and welcome wind. The Square looks like a tenement courtyard. Tumbledown people are asleep on the benches in a friendly forgiveness of each other. And drunks, drunks, drunks, talking to children, to the moon, to everyone going by . . . Bursts of music can be heard from MacDougal Alley, and voices of dancers from the houses with open doors. The church also stands wide open. Into it go the cries of the street children, and out of it come the cries of the half fear-inspiring pastor, who is throwing himself about now, his collar off, sweating and waving his arms, in his baseball sermon.

R. B.

AUTHOR'S CLUB

I had always thought perhaps there would be no poets at all in New York. What I had never suspected was that there would be so many bad ones, or a place like this, as dry and dusty as our own Ateneo in Madrid, in spite of its being on the 15th floor, almost at the altitude of Parnassus.

Tenth-rate men, all of them, cultivating physical resemblances to Poe, to Walt Whitman, to Stevenson, to Mark Twain, letting their soul be burned up with their free cigar, since the two are the same; bushy-haired men who make fun of Robinson, Frost, Masters, Vachel Lindsay, Amy Lowell and who fail to make fun of Poe, Emily Dickinson and Whitman only because they are already dead. And they show me wall after wall of portraits and autographs in holograph, of Bryant, of Aldrich, of Lowell, etc., etc., etc. . . .

. . . I have taken a cigarette from the fumidor, lighted it and thrown it into a corner, on the rug, in order to see if the fire will catch and leave behind it in place of this club of rubbish a high and empty hole, fresh and deep, with clear stars, in the cloudless sky of this April night.

R. B.

WALT WHITMAN

"But do you really want to see Whitman's house instead of Roosevelt's? I've never had this request before!"

The house is tiny and yellow, and next to the railroad track, like the hut of a switchman, in a small green patch of grass, marked out with whitewashed stones, beneath a single tree. Around it, the wide meadow area is open to the wind, which sweeps it, and us, and has polished the simple rough piece of marble which announces to the trains:

TO MARK THE BIRTHPLACE OF
WALT WHITMAN
THE GOOD GRAY POET
BORN MAY 31, 1819
ERECTED BY THE COLONIAL SOCIETY
OF HUNTINGTON IN 1905

Since the farmer doesn't seem to be at home, I walk around the house a couple of times, hoping to see something through the windowlets. Suddenly a man, tall, slow-moving and bearded, wearing a shirt and wide-brimmed hat—like the early photograph of Whitman—comes, from somewhere, and tells me, leaning on his iron bar, that he doesn't know who Whitman was, that he is Polish, that this house is his, and that he does not intend to show it to anyone. Then pulling himself up, he goes inside, through the little door that looks like a toy door.

Solitude and cold. A train goes by, into the wind. The sun, scarlet for an instant, dies behind the low woods, and in the swamp we walk past which is green and faintly blood-colored, innumerable toads are croaking in the enormous silence.

R. B.

LAVENDER WINDOWPANES AND WHITE CURTAINS

Lavender windowpanes! They are like a pedigree of nobility. Boston has many of them and New York has a few, in the old streets around Washington Square, so pleasing, so hospitable, so full of silence! These beautiful panes survive particularly in Boston and are cared for with a haughty, self-interested zeal.

They go back to colonial days. The panes were made with substances which the sunlight over the years has been turning the color of the amethyst, of pansies, of the violet. One feels sure that between the sweet white muslin curtains of those quiet houses, he could glimpse through the violet pane the frail and noble spirit of those days, days of genuine silver and genuine gold, making no hearable sound.

Some of the panes have their violet color almost invisibly, like the flowers and stones I spoke of, and it takes skill simply to see it; others transfer their vague shading to their sister curtains, when the light of the pure sunsets strikes them; finally, by now a few panes are lavender all through, rotten with nobility.

My heart lingers back there with these panes, America, like an amethyst, a pansy, a violet, in the center of the muslin snow. I have been planting that heart for you in the ground beneath the magnolias that the panes reflect, so that each April the pink and white flowers and their odor will surprise the simple Puritan women with their plain clothes, their noble look, and their pale gold hair, coming back at evening, quietly returning to their homes here in those calm spring hours that have made them homesick for earth.

R. B.

NOCTURNE

to Antonio Machado

. . . It is the celestial geometry
of an old astronomer
above the tall city—towers that are
black, slender, small, the end of all. . .

As if, from an ultimate watchtower,
the astrologer was
watching.

                    Exact
signs, fires and colors,
with their shallow and detached secret
in the translucent atmosphere
of deep and blue transparency.

What brightness, what threats,
what positions, what omens,
in the inevitable certainty
of the strange truth! Anatomy
of the sky, with the science
of their function, in itself and for us!

—A sharp cry, lonely, immense,
like a shooting star.—

                    . . . How far
we are from these things,
from that spring evening
—in Washington Square, tranquil and calm—
from those dreams and that love!

                                        D.M. & C.Z.

28

REMORSE

I would cover time for him
with roses so that no one
will remember.

A special rose,
of unforeseen magic
on each solitary hour of gold
or shadow,
precious moment for tragic memories.

There among the divine
and joyful
climbing, rambling roses, crimson and white,
that will not allow any room for the past,
the soul
will intertwine
with the body.

D.M. & C.Z.

CONVEXITIES

The sky turns its back on me,
and so does the sea, and between the nakedness of both,
the day slips along my back.

What is left of the day
is what everyone has said before.
Our three breasts—God!—are open,
against all that faces us,
all that everyone is unaware of,
towards everything!

D.M. & C.Z.

SMOKE AND GOLD

to Enrique and Amparo Granados

So much sea in the yellow moonlight
between us, Spain! And so much sea, tomorrow,
with the dawning sun . . .

                                    . . . Vague ships
sail at daybreak,
mournful sirens sounding there, as though nude,
awake. I hear them say goodbye,
—the solitary moon
dying, broken—O Poe!—over Broadway—
Awake I hear them, with my forehead
pressing the rigid windowpanes; I hear
them say goodbye repeatedly, in my sleep.
—At dawn there is nothing more left than an opening
of cold light in which today is
a black burning bulk—
In the dreams of those who sleep with
the living part of their lives
beside
the part which has died . . .

How far, how far off
from you and me they are and from everything,
—the olive groves at dawn—
When I hear the vigilant word—death!—
within the harmony of the soul
—an immense sea of grief and joy—
by the yellow light
of this setting and lonely moon, Spain!

                                              D.M. & C.Z.

NOCTURNE

The ship, slow and swift at once, conquers the water
but not the sky.
The blue remains behind, opening into living silver,
and once more is in front.
Fixed, the mast sways, always returning
—like the hour hand turning in even numbers
on the clock face—
to the stars themselves,
hour after hour, black and green.
One's body, dreaming, returns
to the country it's from, coming from the world
it does not belong to. One's soul remains and
continues, always, through its eternal domain.

                                                    D.M. & C.Z.

Intelligence, give me
the exact name of things!
. . . Let my word be
the thing itself,
newly created again by my soul.
So all those who don't know them
can go through me, to things;
so all those who have already forgotten them,
can go through me, to things;
so all those who love them,
can go through me, to things . . .
Intelligence, give me
the exact name, and your name,
and theirs and mine, for things!

                                                    D.M. & C.Z.

Sleep is like a bridge
that stretches from today to tomorrow.
Underneath, like a dream,
water flows.

D. M.

OCEANS

I have a feeling that my boat
has struck, down there in the depths,
against a great thing.
                              And nothing
happens! Nothing . . . Silence . . . Waves . . .

—Nothing happens? Or has everything happened,
and are we standing now, quietly, in the new life?

R. B.

I am like a distracted child,
who they drag by the hand
through the fiesta of the world.

My eyes cling, sadly
to things . . .

And what sorrow when they tear me away!

D. M.

To the bridge of love,
old stone between tall cliffs
     —eternal meeting place, red evening—,
I come with my heart.
     —My beloved is only water,
that always passes away, and does not deceive,
that always passes away, and does not change,
that always passes away, and does not end.

J. W.

ROAD

They all are asleep, below.
                                    Above, awake,
the helmsman and I.

He, watching the compass needle, lord
of the bodies, with their keys turned
in the locks. I, with my eyes
toward the infinite, guiding
the open treasures of the souls.

R. B.

I pulled on the reins,
I turned the horse
of the dawn,
and I came in to life, pale.

Oh how they looked at me,
the flowers of my dream,
insane,
lifting their arms to the moon!

R. B.

At first she came to me pure,
dressed only in her innocence;
and I loved her as we love a child.

Then she began putting on
clothes she picked up somewhere;
and I hated her, without knowing it.

She gradually became a queen,
the jewelry was blinding . . .
What bitterness and rage!

. . . She started going back toward nakedness.
And I smiled.

Soon she was back to the single shift
of her old innocence.
I believed in her a second time.

Then she took off the cloth
and was entirely naked . . .
Naked poetry, always mine,
that I have loved my whole life!

R. B.

I am not I.
            I am this one
walking beside me whom I do not see,
whom at times I manage to visit,
and whom at other times I forget;
who remains calm and silent while I talk,
and forgives, gently, when I hate,
who walks where I am not,
who will remain standing when I die.

R. B.

34

LIFE

What I used to regard as a glory shut in my face,
was a door, opening
toward this clarity:
    Country without a name:

Nothing can destroy it, this road
of doors, opening, one after another,
always toward reality:
    Life without calculation!

J. W.

THE POEM

I pulled out the plant by the roots
still dripping with the dew
    of early morning.
How it watered the earth
fragrant and moist.
What rain! What blindness of stars
in my face and eyes!

D. M.

NEW COLD

New cold: rooster crowing.
Thunder and moon: child weeping.
Lonely street: dog leaving.
Last night still: man thinking.

D. M.

35

DAWN

Daybreak brings with it
that sad feeling of arrival by train
at a station that isn't one's own.

How disagreeable are the thoughts
of a day one knows is transitory!
— Oh, my life! —

Above, with the dawn, a child's crying . . .

D. M.

TO DANTE

Your sonnet is like
a nude and chaste woman
who set me on her lap,
embracing me with her celestial arms.

Afterward, I dreamed of it and her.
It was a fountain,
with two jets arching into a first
basin, which, in turn, pours
in thin streams into two others . . .

D.M. & C.Z.

IDEAL EPITAPH FOR A SAILOR

One must search the heavens
to find your grave.
Your death is raining from the stars.
The tombstone does not weigh on you;
it is a universe of dreams.
Unknown, you are
in everything—sky, sea, and land—dead.

D.M. & C.Z.

The ship, solid and black,
enters the clear blackness
of the great harbor.
                    Quiet and cold.
                              —The people waiting
are still asleep, dreaming,
and warm, far away and still stretched out in this
dream, perhaps . . .

How real our watch is, beside the dream
of doubt the others had! How sure it is, compared
to their troubled dream about us!
                              Quiet. Silence.
Silence which is breaking up at dawn
will speak differently.

R. B.

What an immense rip
in my life and in all things,
in order to be with my entire self,
in everything;
in order to never cease being,
with my entire self, in everything.

D.M. & C.Z.

FACING THE VIRGIN SHADOW

I'm always penetrating you,
but you are always a virgin,
shadow; like that day
in which I first came
calling to your secret,
charged with a boundless passion.

Dark, full virgin
overripe with deep rainbows
that can scarcely be seen; all
black, with the sublime
stars, which do not come
(up) to discover you!

D.M. & C.Z.

38

FIGURATIONS

Oh, days coloring the night:
dawns—golden dahlias covered with dew—
from the tunnel of dreams;
zeniths—magic roofs in flames—
from the cave of sleep;
—pheasants against the scarlet sunset—
west winds from the prison of illusion;
—involuntary and slow beauty, always
there for the unaware,
and for the surprised; the only life!—

D.M. & C.Z.

MEMORY—4

O secret memories
off the roads
of all my other memories!

Memories that one night
suddenly sprang forth again,
like a rose in the desert,
like a star at noon,
—great passion of cold forgetfulness—
boundaries of a
great life,
scarcely lived at all!

Path
always dry and arid;
sudden wonder
of a unique spring,
of forgotten memories!

D.M. & C.Z.

MEMORY—5

The river flows beneath
my soul, undermining me.
I can hardly maintain my
strength. The sky doesn't
sustain me. Even the stars
deceive me; they are not
above, but below, down there in the depths . . .

Am I here? I will be!
I will be transformed into a wave
on the river of memory . . .

With you, running water!

D.M. & C.Z.

TO BELOVED OLD AGE

If only your memory
of me were this blue May
sky, completely filled with
the pure stars of my acts!

If my acts were identical, like them; all pure,
clear, good, tranquil, just like the stars!

Below, I see you smile in dreams
—dreams of your memories of my life!—

D.M. & C.Z.

UPHILL

Immense flowering almond tree,
your crown white in the full silence of the moonlight,
your black trunk in the total stillness of the shadows.
As I climb up the steep rock towards you,
I feel your huge trunk sink
into the deepest recesses of my flesh,
your stars filling the sky with my soul.

D.M. & C.Z.

LIGHT AND WATER

The light above —golden, orange, green
among the vague clouds.

Ah, trees without leaves,
roots in water,
branches in light!

Underneath, the water —green, orange, golden
among the vague mist.

Among the vague mist, among the vague clouds,
light and water; what magic they vanish!

D. M.

SONG

Above the bird sings
and below the water sings.
Above and below
my soul is opening.

The bird shakes the star
and water rocks the flower.
Above and below
my soul is trembling.

D. M.

Even though my soul fits so wonderfully
inside my body—
like a clear idea
in a line perfect for it—
nevertheless it has to abandon the body
eventually, leaving it like some academic's line,
hollow and stiff!

R. B.

Butterfly of light,
beauty leaves when I arrive
at its rose.

I run, blindly, after it . . .
Almost catching it here and there . . .

All that's left in my hand
is the shape of its flight!

D.M. & C.Z.

FULL MOON

The door is open,
the cricket singing.
Are you going around naked
in the fields?

Like an immortal water,
going in and out of everything.
Are you going around naked
in the air?

The basil is not asleep,
the ant is busy.
Are you going around naked
in the house?

R. B.

DUSK

Dusk. Great clouds smother the village.
The streetlights are sad and drowsy.
And the yellow moon wanders
    between water and wind.

An odor rises from the drenched countryside.
A greenish star appears behind
    the old bell tower.
The seven o'clock coach passes . . . Dogs bark . . .

Going out on the road I feel the cold moon
on my face . . . near the white cemetery
on the hill, the tall black pines weep.

D. M.

DAWN OUTSIDE THE CITY WALLS

You can see the face of everything, and it is
    white—
plaster, nightmare, adobe, anemia, cold—
turned to the east. Oh closeness to life!
Hardness of life! Like something
in the body that is animal—root, slag-ends—
with the soul still not set well there—
and mineral and vegetable!
Sun standing stiffly against man,
against the sow, the cabbages, the mud wall!
—False joy, because you are merely
in time, as they say, and not in the soul!

The entire sky is taken up
by moist and steaming heaps,
a horizon of dung piles.
Sour remains, here and there,
of the night. Slices
of the green moon, half-eaten,
crystal bits from false stars,
plaster, the paper ripped off, still faintly
sky-blue. The birds
not really awake yet, in the raw moon,
streetlight nearly out.
Mob of beings and things!
—A true sadness, because you are really deep
in the soul, as they say, not in time at all!

R. B.

44

PEACE

When at sunrise
the scarlet bellflowers open
to the golden moon,
you will no longer be home,
naked, white shadow.

—You will be nobly
at ease and smiling in
cheerful surprise,
contented with your fate
that makes you indifferent,
in the face of life and death.—

The day will gradually lighten
with a melancholy light;
the green, cold breeze
will fill the empty roof,
like pouring water from above.

. . . And one will have to get up
and scurry about doing the morning things,
and will see and hear everywhere
the shouts, the running back and forth, the boasting,
—the sun on one's poor flesh and blood!—,
the bewildered, bitter ugliness.

D.M. & C.Z.

WITH THE ROSES

No, this pleasant afternoon
I cannot stay inside;
this free afternoon
I must go out in the air.

Into the laughing air
opening through the trees,
thousands of loves,
profound and waving.

The roses wait for me
bathing their flesh.
Nothing can keep me here;
I will not stay inside!

D. M.

FULL CONSCIOUSNESS

You are carrying me, full consciousness, god that
        has desires,
all through the world.
                    Here, in this third sea,
I almost hear your voice; your voice, the wind,
filling entirely all movements;
eternal colors and eternal light,
sea colors and sea lights.

Your voice of white fire
in the universe of water, the ship, the sky,
marking out the roads with delight,
engraving for me with a blazing light my firm orbit:
a black body
with the glowing diamond in its center.

R. B.

I wish that all my poems
could be like the sky at night.
The truth of the moment, without history.

That, like the sky, they would yield at every
        moment all things,
with all their stars.
Not childhood, or youth, or age could rob them
or cast a spell on their immense beauty.

A tremor, a flash, the music present and total.
The tremor, the flash, the music in my head,
the sky in my heart. The naked book!

D. M.

PLATERO AND I

Translated by
Antonio T. de Nicolas

SHORT PROLOGUE

Some people believe that I wrote *Platero and I* for children, that this is a book for children.

No. In 1913, the editor of *La Lectura*, who knew I was writing this book, asked me to advance a few of its most idyllic pages for its "youth series." Then, changing my idea momentarily, I wrote this prologue:

A NOTE TO THOSE GROWNUPS WHO MIGHT
READ THIS BOOK TO CHILDREN:

This short book, where joy and sadness are twins, like the ears of Platero, was written for . . . I have no idea for whom! . . . For whomever lyric poets write. . . . Now that it goes to the children, I do not add nor remove a single comma. That's it!

"Wherever there are children"—Novalis used to say—"there is a Golden Age." Well, it is within this Golden Age, which is like a spiritual island fallen from the skies, that the heart of the poet walks, and it finds itself there so at home that its most cherished wish would be not to have to ever abandon it.

Island of grace, of freshness and of joy, Golden Age of children; I always could find you in my life, a sea of mourning; let your breeze lend me its lyre high and sometimes senseless like the trill of the lark in the white sun of the morning!

I have never written nor will I ever write anything for children, because I believe that the child can read the books that grownups read, with some few exceptions that come to everyone's mind. There are of course exceptions too for men and for women.

—Juan Ramon Jimenez

PLATERO

Platero is small, fluffy, soft; so soft on the outside that one would say he is all cotton, that he carries no bones. Only the jet-dark mirrors of his eyes are hard as two scarabs of black crystal.

I let him loose and he runs to the meadow; warmly, hardly touching them, he brushes his nose against the tiny pink, sky-blue and golden yellow flowers. . . . I call him sweetly: "Platero?" and he comes to me at a gay little trot as though he were laughing, I do not know within what fancy world of jingles.

He eats whatever I give him. He likes oranges, tangerines, muscatel grapes, all amber, purple figs with their crystalline drops of honey. . . .

He is tender and cuddly, as a little boy, as a little girl . . . but inside he is strong and dry as a stone. When I ride him on Sunday through the last alleyways of the town, the men from the fields, dressed neatly and slow moving, stand still watching him.

"He's got steel."

Steel, yes. Steel and moon silver at the same time.

GAMES AT DUSK

When, in the village at twilight, Platero and I enter, shivering with cold, through the purple shadows of the wretched alley which leads to the dry river bed, poor children play at frightening one another, pretending to be beggars. One throws a sack over his head, another says he cannot see, another plays lame. . . .

Later, in one of those sudden changes that happen with children, and since they are really wearing shoes and are dressed, and their mothers (only they know how) have managed to feed them, they think themselves to be princes:

"My father has a silver watch."

"And mine a horse."

"And mine a shotgun."

A watch that will rise at dawn. A shotgun that will not kill hunger. A horse that will ride towards poverty.

They then form a circle. Amid so much blackness a little girl with a thin voice, a thread of liquid crystal in the shadows, tunefully sings, like a princess:

"I'm the young widow of the Count of Ore. . . . "

Yes, yes! Sing. Dream, poor children! Soon, at the first blush of your youth, spring will frighten you, like a beggar in winter's guise.

"Come on, Platero."

THE ECLIPSE

We put our hands in our pockets without meaning to, and the forehead feels the delicate fluttering of the fresh shadow, as when one enters a thick pine forest. The hens start to gather in their sheltered roost, one by one. Around us the countryside darkens its own green, as if the purple veil from the main altar were covering it. The distant sea appears white to the eye and a few stars shine dimly. How the terraces change white for white! Those of us standing on them shout witticisms to one another, good or bad, looking small and dark, in that brief silence of the eclipse.

We look at the sun through a variety of things: opera glasses, field glasses, a bottle, smoked glass; and from everywhere: from the upper balcony, from the ladder in the corral, from the window in the barn, from the grating of the patio through its blue and scarlet glass. . . .

The hiding of the sun, which a moment earlier had made everything two, three, a hundred times larger and better with its complexities of light and gold, now, without the long transition of the twilight, leaves everything looking lonely and poor, as if it had traded its gold, first for silver and then for copper. The village is like a penny, dull and of no value. How sad and small the streets, the squares, the towers, the paths on the mountains!

Platero, down there in the corral, seems less real, different and plastic, a different donkey. . . .

KINDERGARTEN

If you would come, Platero, with the other children to kindergarten, you would learn your ABCs and you might even learn to write your name. You would learn as much as the donkey of the wax figurines—the friend of the little mermaid of the sea, who always appears crowned with cloth flowers, through the mirror that shows her, all pink, flesh and gold, in her green element—more even than the doctor and the priest of Palos, Platero.

But though you are only four years old, you are so big and so ungainly! In which little chair would you sit? At which desk would you write? What book or what pen would be sufficient for you? In which part of the choir would you sing, let us say, the Creed?

No, Dona Domitila—always dressed with her habit of Father Jesus of Nazareth, all purple with a yellow rope, like Reyes, the fishmonger—she would most probably keep you for two hours on your knees in a corner of the sycamore patio, or she would hit you with her long and dry reed on the hooves, or she would eat the quince jelly of your *merienda*, or she would hang a burning paper from your tail and she would make your ears as red and hot as the ears of the harness-maker's son when it is about to rain. . . . No, Platero, no. Come with me. I will show you the flowers and the stars and no one will laugh at you as they laugh at slow children. And they are not going to put on you, as if you were what they call a donkey, the big hat with painted large blue and red eyes, like those of the river barges, with ears twice as large as yours.

FIGS

The foggy and crude dawn was good to the figs, and at the stroke of six we went to the Rica to eat them.

Under the large century-old fig trees, whose gray trunks entwined their opulent thighs in the cold shade as under a skirt, the night was still asleep; and the wide leaves—that Adam and Eve wore—treasured a fine texture of tiny dew pearls which whitened their soft green. From within that green inside, one could see, through the low exuberant emerald, the dawn, which more alive each time was turning pink the uncolored veils of the East.

. . . We were running like mad to see who would get first to each fig tree. Rocillo caught the first leaf of one with me, in an exuberance of laughter and palpitations—"Touch here," and she would put my hand with hers over her heart, her young breast moving up and down like a minute, captive wave—Adela, fat and small, could hardly run and she was getting angry from where she stood far away. I picked a few ripe figs for Platero and put them on the seat of an old grapevine so that he would not get bored. Adela started the shooting, angry at her own clumsiness, with laughter in her mouth and tears in her eyes. She smashed a fig on my forehead. Rocillo and I followed suit, and even more than through the mouth, we ate figs through the eyes, through the nose, through the sleeves, through the nape, in a sharp and endless shouting that would fall, with the aimless figs, in the vineyards, fresh with the morning. A fig hit Platero, and he became the target of our madness. Since the poor creature could not defend himself or retaliate, I took his side; and a soft and blue deluge criss-crossed the pure air in all directions, like fast-moving missiles. A double laughter, fallen and tired, expressed from the ground the feminine fatigue.

THE GELDING

He was black, with a sheen of scarlet, green and blue, all silvery like the beetles and the crows. A bright fire would flash at times in his young eyes, as is the pot of Ramona, the chestnut vendor in the Plaza del Marques. How his brief trotting steps clattered when, coming from the sands of La Friseta, he entered triumphantly, a champion on the cobblestones of the Calle Nueva! How quick, how nervous, how keen he was, with his small head and his lean legs!

Nobly he passed by the low doorway of the wine cellar—blacker even than he against the red sun shining from the Castle, which was a dazzling background to the wine caves—his gait easy, and ready to play with everything. Afterward, jumping over the pine log, threshold of the door, he filled the green corral with joy and with the clamor of hens, doves and sparrows. There, four men, their hairy arms crossed over their colored shirts, awaited him. They led him under the pepper tree. After a harsh and brief struggle, first kindly, then fiercely, they threw him down on the manure, and with all of them sitting on him, Darbon performed his duty, putting an end to the horse's poignant and magical beauty.

"Thy unus'd beauty must be tomb'd with thee
Which, used, lives th' executor to be"

as Shakespeare wrote to his friend.

The colt, now a horse, was left soft, sweating, exhausted and sad. One man alone was enough to get him up, and covering him with a blanket, he led him, slowly, down the street.

Poor vain cloud, a bolt of lightning only yesterday, tempered and firm! He was like a book with its binding falling apart. It seemed that he was no longer touching the earth, that between his hooves and the stones a new insulating element isolated him, leaving him for no reason like an uprooted tree, like a memory, on that violent, whole and round spring morning.

THE TERRACE

You, Platero, have never been up to the terrace. You cannot know what deep breathing swells the chest when, on coming out of the dark wooden staircase, one feels burned in the midday sun, flooded with blue as if one were beside the sky itself, blinded by the whiteness of the lime with which, as you know, the brick floor is painted so that the water arrives clean from the clouds to the cistern.

How enchanting the roof terrace! The bells of the tower are ringing in our breast, at the level of our heart which is beating strongly; far, in the vineyards, one can see the hoes shining with a spark of silver and sun; one can see over everything: the other terraces; the corrals, where people, unaware, toil at their own work—the chair-maker, the painter, the barrel-maker; the leafy patches of the large corrals, with the goat or the bull; the cemetery where at times one may see arriving an unnoticed third-class funeral, small, tight and black; windows with a young girl in a slip combing her hair, carefree and singing; the river, with the boat which never seems to arrive; barns where a lonely musician practices his trumpet, or where violent love, round, blind and secretive, burns the hay. . . .

The house disappears like a basement. How strange the ordinary life below appears through the panes of a skylight: words, noises, even the garden itself, which is so beautiful when in it; you, Platero, drinking in the cistern, not seeing me, or playing, like a fool, with a sparrow or a turtle!

RETURN

We were both returning laden from the woods, Platero with marjoram and I with yellow lilies.

The April evening was waning. All that in the sunset had been gold crystal was now silver crystal, a plain and luminous allegory of crystal lilies. Later the vast sky was like a transparent sapphire turning to emerald. I was feeling sad. . . .

From the slope, the village tower crowned with shining tiles appeared in the rising of the pure hour like a monument. From near, it looked like Sevilla's Giralda seen from far away, and my nostalgia for the cities sharpened by the spring, found in it a melancholy comfort.

Return . . . where? From where? For what? . . . But the lilies I was carrying with me became fragrant in the warm freshness of the arriving evening; their scent grew more intense and at the same time more vague, coming from the flower while the flower could not be seen, a flower made of scent only, intoxicating the body and the soul from the solitary shadow.

"Soul of mine, lily in the shadows!" I said.

And I suddenly thought of Platero, who, though walking under me, I had forgotten as if he were my own body.

DON JOSE, THE PRIEST

There you have him, Platero, sanctified and speaking as if he had honey in his mouth. But the one who is really always an angel is his donkey, a true lady.

I believe you saw him one day in his orchard, in sailor's trousers, wide hat, hurling insults and stones at the little children who were stealing his oranges. A thousand times you have seen, on Fridays, poor Balthasar, his caretaker, dragging his hernia that looks like a circus ball, along the road to the village, to sell his wretched brooms, or to pray with the poor for the dead of the rich. . . .

I never heard any man use worse language, nor shake the high heavens with such swear words. It is true, no doubt, that he knows, or so he says in his five o'clock mass, where Heaven is and how everything is arranged there. . . . The tree, the soil, the water, the wind, the fire, these things, each so graceful, so soft, so fresh, so pure, so alive, seem to serve him only as examples of disorder, hardness, frigidity, violence, decay. Daily all the stones in his orchard spend the night in a different spot, shot in furious hostility against birds, washerwomen, children and flowers. When time to pray comes, all turns around. The silence of Don Jose may be heard in the silence of the fields. He puts on a cassock, cloak and priestly hat, and with his eyes unfocused he enters the dark village on his slow donkey, like Jesus going to his death.

THE CISTERN

Look at it, Platero, full with the last rains. It has no echo, nor can you see, as when it is low, down there in its depth, the balcony with sun, a polychrome jewel behind the yellow and blue crystals of the glass roof. You have never gone down in the cistern, Platero, but I have. I went down once when they emptied it years ago. It has a long gallery and then a tiny room. When I entered it, the candle I was carrying went out and a salamander jumped into my hand. Two terrible chills crossed my breast like two swords crossing, like two crossbows beneath a skull. . . .

The whole village is undermined by cisterns and tunnels. The largest cistern is in the patio of the Salto del Lobo, in the square of the ancient citadel of the Castle. The best is this one in my house, which, as you can see, has a curbstone carved from a single piece of white marble. The tunnel under the church goes all the way to the vineyard at Los Puntales and there it opens to the fields, by the river. No one has dared follow the tunnel under the hospital to the end because it never ends. . . . I remember, when I was a child, the long rainy nights, when the sobbing sound of the round waters flowing from the terrace to the cistern kept me awake. Then in the morning, we would go excitedly to see up to what point the water had risen. When it was up to the rim, as it is today, what excitement, what shouts, what wonder!

. . . Well, Platero. Now I am going to give you a bucketful of this pure and fresh water, the same bucketful that Villegas, the poor Villegas, whose body was already charred from too much cognac and brandy, would drink in one draught. . . .

61

THE LITTLE CART

In the large stream which the rain had swollen up to the vineyard, we found an old little cart stuck, wholly lost beneath its load of grass and oranges. A little girl, her clothes torn and dirty, was crying by one of the wheels, trying to help with the push of her little, budding chest a small donkey, much smaller, oh! and thinner than Platero. And the little donkey was struggling against the wind, trying in vain to pull the cart from the mud, at each sobbing cry of the little girl. His effort was in vain, as that of courageous children, as the flight of those tired summer breezes, that fall in a faint among the flowers.

I gave Platero a little pat and, as best as I could, I hitched him to the little cart in front of the pitiful donkey. I forced him, then, with a loving command, and Platero, in one pull, dragged the little cart and the donkey from the hole in the mud and pulled them up the slope.

What a smile on the little girl's face! It was as if the evening sun, while setting among rain clouds and breaking in yellow crystals, was lighting up a dawn behind her soiled tears.

In her tearful joy, she offered me two perfect oranges, delicate, heavy, round. I took them, grateful, and then I gave one to the weak little donkey, as sweet consolation; the other, to Platero, as golden prize.

BREAD

I told you, Platero, that Moguer's soul is wine, didn't I? No, Moguer's soul is bread. Moguer is like a loaf of wheat bread, white inside, like the crumbs, and gold outside—oh, brown sun!—like the soft crust. At noon when the sun burns most, the whole town begins to smoke and smell of pines and warm bread. The whole town opens its mouth; a large mouth eating a large bread. Bread mixes with everything: with oil, gazpacho, cheese and grapes, to give the taste of kisses to the wine, the soup, the ham, to itself, bread with bread. All alone, like hope, or with some dream. . . .

Those delivering the bread arrive trotting on their horses, stop at each half-opened door, clap their hands and shout: "The bread maaaan! . . ." One can hear the hard, tender sound of the large loaves against the rolls, or the flat loaf against the cakes, as they fall in the baskets that naked arms lift. . . .

And the poor children, always on time, ring the little bells of the gates or knock the latches of the big doors, crying for a long time towards the inside:

"Please, one little bit of bread! . . . "

DARBON

Darbon, Platero's doctor, is as large as a piebald ox, as red as a watermelon. He weighs three hundred pounds. His age, according to him, is three score.

When he talks, sounds are missing, as in an old piano; at times instead of words his mouth lets out bursts of air. These mumblings are accompanied by nodding of the head, waving hands, dodderings, clearings of the throat and of saliva into the handkerchief; so you could not ask for more. A pleasant concert to precede supper.

He has not one tooth or molar left, and eats almost nothing but breadcrumbs which he first kneads in his hand. He makes a ball, and up to the red mouth it goes! There he keeps it, rolling it about, for an hour. Then another ball, and another. He chews with his gums, and his chin reaches up to his hawked nose.

I say he is as large as the piebald ox. Standing at the doorway by the bench, he covers the whole house. But he is tender like a child with Platero and if he sees a flower or a tiny bird, he gives a sudden laugh, opening the whole of his mouth in long sustained laughter, which always ends in tears. Then, calm once more, he looks towards the old cemetery for a long time:

"My little girl, my poor little girl. . . . "

FRIENDSHIP

We understand each other very well. I let him follow his whim, and he always takes me where I want to go. Platero knows that when we reach the pine in La Corona, I like to go up to its trunk and caress it and look at the sky through its enormous and clear top. He knows I delight in following the little footpath which leads through the lawns to the old fuente; that it is a treat for me to see the river from the pine-filled hill, evoking classical scenes with its tall little forest. Should I doze, confident on his back, my eyes will always open on some such pleasant sights.

I deal with Platero as if he were a child. If the path grows rough and I become slightly heavy on him, I alight to help him. I kiss him, I trick him, I tease him. He well understands that I love him, and he bears me no grudge. He is so much like me that I have come to believe he dreams my own dreams.

Platero has surrendered to me like a passionate adolescent. He protests at nothing. I know I am his happiness. He even flees from other donkeys and from other men. . . .

THE TREE IN THE CORRAL

This tree, Platero, this acacia that I myself planted, this green flame that kept on growing spring after spring, and that right now shades us with her abundant and healthy leaves roasting with the setting sun, was, while I lived in this house, the best sustenance of my poems. Any of her branches, decked in emerald in April or in gold in October, would refresh, just by looking at her for awhile, my forehead, like the purest hand of a muse. How delicate, how elegant, how beautiful she was!

Today, Platero, she owns almost the whole corral. How huge she has become! I do not know if she would remember me. To me, she looks different. During all this time that I was forgetting her, almost as if she did not exist, spring had been transforming her, year after year, according to its whim, not in a way pleasing to my feelings.

Today she means nothing to me, in spite of being a tree, and a tree which I planted. Any tree that we caress for the first time fills our hearts with meaning, Platero. A tree that we have loved so much, that we have known so well, doesn't mean anything to us when we see it again, Platero. It is sad: But it is useless to say any more. No, I cannot, in this union of acacia and the setting sun, look any longer at my hanging lyre. The graceful branch does not bring any verses nor does the inner shine of the tree-top quicken my thought. And here, where so many times I came from life with a dream of musical solitude, fresh and scented, I feel ill at ease, and cold and I want to run away, as I used to, in the old days, from the casino, the bar or the theater, Platero.

THE RIVER

Look Platero, what they have done to the river with those mines, those bad hearts and bad politics. This afternoon its red water can hardly catch here and there, all covered with violet and yellow mud, the setting sun, and through its bed nothing can sail but toy boats. What misery!

Not long ago the great ships of the wine merchants, catboats, brigs, feluccas—El Lobo, La Joven Eloisa, the San Cayetano, which belonged to my father and was piloted by poor Quintero, La Estrella, my uncle's, captained by Picon—darted the sky of San Juan with a joyful confusion of their masts—their main masts so amazed the children!—or they would go to Malaga, or Cadiz or Gibraltar, almost sinking in the river with such heavy loads of wine. By sailing amongst them the fishing boats would make the traffic more complicated with their eyes, saints, names painted in green, blue, white, yellow, pink. . . . And the fishermen would bring up to the village sardines, oysters, eels, sole, crabs. . . . The copper for Riô Tinto has poisoned everything. And thank goodness, Platero, that with the pollution of the rich, the poor may eat the miserable fish of today. . . . But the feluccas, the brigs, the catboats have all been lost.

What misery, though! The statue of Christ is no longer able to see the movement of the waters with the tides! What remains—feeble thread of blood from a corpse, tattered and dry beggar—the lifeless stream of the river, the color of rust like this red sunset against which La Estrella—dismantled, black and rotten, her damaged keel upturned—outlines her burned hull like the skeleton of a fish, and all she is good for is for the children of the customs guards to play in her as the anxiety of premonitions plays in my poor heart.

THE OLD FOUNTAIN

Always white against the always green pine grove; rose or blue in the dawn, being white; gold or mauve in the afternoon, being white; green or blue in the night, being white; the Old Fountain, Platero, where you have seen me lost in thought for so long, holds within it, like a code or a tomb, the whole of the world's elegy, that is, the feeling of the true life.

In it I have seen the Parthenon, the Pyramids, all the cathedrals. Each time a fountain, a mausoleum, a portico stirred me with the insistent permanence of its beauty, its image mixed in my dreamy state with the image of the Old Fountain.

From her I went to everything. To her I came from everything. She is so set on her own spot in such a way, she is so eternal in her harmonious simplicity, the color and the light are so completely her own, that one could take from her in one's own hand, like one does with her water, the whole spring of life. Bocklin painted her over Greece; Fray Luis translated her; Beethoven flattered her with joyful weeping; Michelangelo gave her to Rodin.

She is the cradle and she is the wedding; she is the song and she is the sonnet; she is reality and she is joy; she is death.

She is dead there, Platero, tonight, like flesh of marble between the dark and white flowing greenness; she is dead, flowing from my soul the water of my own eternity.

PINE NUTS

There she comes, through the sun of the Calle Nueva, the little girl with the pine nuts. She brings them raw and toasted. I am going to buy from her, for you and for me, ten cents worth of toasted pine nuts, Platero.

November alternates winter and summer with golden and blue days. The sun stings and the veins swell like leeches, round and blue. . . . Along the white, peaceful and clean streets passes the linen man from La Mancha, his gray bundle over his shoulder; the hardware man from Lucena, all wrapped in yellow light, sounding his bell that catches the sun in each sound. . . . And, slow, close to the wall, drawing a long line in charcoal on the whitewash, there is the little girl of La Arena, half bent with her load, announcing loudly and with feeling:

"The toasted piiiiine nuuuutssss!"

People in love eat them together at the doorsteps, exchanging, amid flaming smiles, chosen nuts. Children going to school break the kernel on the doorways with a stone as they keep moving. . . . I remember that as a child, we used to go to the orange grove of Mariano by Los Arroyos on winter afternoons. We used to take with us a handkerchief full of toasted pine nuts with kernels, and in my dreams I longed to carry that knife with which we would break them; it was a pocket knife with a handle of mother-of-pearl carved in the shape of a fish, with two tiny, opposite ruby eyes through which one could see the Eiffel Tower. . . .

What a pleasant taste toasted pine nuts leave in the mouth, Platero. They give such vigor, such optimism! One feels secure with them in the sun of the cold season as if one had already become an immortal monument, and one walks about noisily and one carries one's winter clothes without feeling their weight, and one even feels the temptation of locking wrists with Leon, Platero, or with El Manquito, the attendant of the coaches. . . .

THE FABLE

Since childhood, Platero, I have had an instinctive horror of apologists, as well as the church, the Guardia Civil, bullfighters and accordions. The poor animals, forced to speak stupidities through the mouths of fable makers, seemed to be as hateful as in the silence of the stinking showcases in the museums of Natural History. Each word they said, I mean that a gentleman with a cold, hoarse voice and yellow-looking would say, seemed to me like a crystal eye, a wire in a wing, a prop of a false branch. Later, when I saw trained animals in the circus of Huelva and of Sevilla, the fable which had remained, like the papers and the prizes, forgotten in the abandoned school, returned like an unpleasant nightmare of my adolescence.

Later on as a man, Platero, a maker of fables, Jean de la Fontaine, of whom you have heard me talk so often, reconciled me with talking animals; and one of his verses, at times, would sound to me like the true voice of the rook, the dove, or the goat. But I always left unread the moral of the story: that dry tale, that ash, that fallen feather at the end.

It is obvious, Platero, that you are not a donkey in the common sense of the word, nor in accordance with the definition of the Dictionary of the Spanish Academy of Letters. You are truly as I know you are, and as I understand you. You have your language and not mine, as I do not have the language of the rose nor does she have that of the nightingale. Therefore, do not be afraid that I would ever make you, as you might have thought by looking at my books, a charlatan hero of a little fable braiding your sonorous expression with that of the fox or the oriole, to draw, in italics, the cold and vain moral of the apologist. No, Platero. . . .